In His Eyes

Sarah Katreen Hoggatt

Spirit Water Publications
Salem, Oregon

IN HIS EYES

Third Printing

SPIRIT WATER PUBLICATIONS
P.O. Box 7522
Salem, Oregon 97303

Library of Congress Catalog Card Number: 2005909704

ISBN-13: 978-0-9729460-1-8
ISBN-10: 0-9729460-1-2

Printed and bound by:
Gorham Printing
3718 Mahoney Drive
Centralia, WA 98531

Cover Art by Emily Cahal
Cover Design by Janelle Wheeler Olivarez
Illustrated by ClaraLee Esther

For additional copies, contact Spirit Water Publications at
www.SpiritWaterPublications.com

Manufactured in the United States of America

Dedication

For you God in whose eyes
is held the vastness of the universe,
eternal life-giving hope,
and truth that never dies.
May my thirsty soul always long to
seek and rest in what I find expressed
in your eyes and to drink deeply
of the living water you pour out from them.
You are my deepest love,
therefore, I dedicate this to you.

Contents

Chapter 6: Companions for the Journey

Chapter 7: Voices of Intimate Prayer

Acknowledgements

The publishing of this book has been a community effort, one in which I have been extraordinarily blessed and humbled. A special heartfelt thank you goes out to the following people:

To ClaraLee Esther for the beautiful illustrations gracing these pages. You have been a joy to work with on this project and I am so grateful to God for bringing us together in his divine plan. Your warmth, encouragement, and skill, have all been valuable contributions of inestimable worth and I thank you dearly for making room in your heart for this book and for me.

To Rebekah Borah for once again being the brilliant graphic artist and treasured friend you have always been to me. I am still amazed at what you can do with a couple of computer files and cheese crackers. To work with you again on this kind of project has been a delight I will always treasure. Also, a very special thank you to Earl, Lydia, Stephanie, and Charlotte Borah for giving up time with your wife and mother so we could work on laying out this book. Your hugs and our conversations over canned spaghetti rings and cheesy poufs has made this time truly memorable.

To Ryan and Laurie Canney for all of your outstanding editing. Your enthusiasm for this project and the warmth of our friendship has been a great encouragement to me. It is because of your many correction marks, quality feedback, and thought provoking ideas that this book has turned out so well. Thank you for all of the late nights, long talks, and hilarious story telling. Huzzah!

To Emily Cahal for giving me the honor of having your beautiful photographic art on the cover and for shocking me with what you can do in Photoshop. The journey of our friendship truly *has* been a blessing in itself. Thank you for the time together and for sharing with me the wisdom you've learned.

To Janelle Wheeler Olivarez who designed the cover so beautifully. Thank you for your expertise and your time. I am grateful to you for sharing them both.

To Adria Farina-Miller for walking with me on my journey of faith, for speaking the words of God into my life as you held up

Christ's light, and for keeping me accountable as I worked on this book. From my soul to yours, thank you for the tears, the laughter, and for all of the prayerful silences in between when we drank deeply of the Holy Spirit's intimacy. These words would not have had the same rich depth without you.

To the community at George Fox Evangelical Seminary for guiding and loving me as I have learned more than I ever dreamed of about ministry and spiritual formation and for listening to these poems and supporting me as I wrote them. My heart overflows with joy when I think of how much you have all added to my life and I am so honored to have known such an extraordinary group of people after God's own heart. Here is to all the lunches, study groups, prayers, jokes, times of shared pain and delight that we have shared before his throne.

To my friends and family for encouraging my gift of writing and for supporting me along the way. The love you have given me has moved me deeply for it is a beautiful thing and I am richly blessed to know you all. Thank you for not only reading over some of these poems and giving me suggestions, but also for all of the inspiration I drew from you.

To you, the readers of this book for asking not long after you finished reading the first one, how long you had to wait until the second was available. I am truly humbled that you would invite me into your lives in such a way as this. It has been your faces and your words God has brought before me as I wrote what you are about to read. May you find in these pages the voice of God and may he touch you in ways he never has before.

Lastly and most importantly, thank you God for loving me more than I will ever realize and for guiding me as I have written this book. You are forever beyond human expression but I hope these words in some small way give you the glory you so richly deserve. Thank you for giving me your peace when I needed it, for stretching me as I have grown in your presence, and for always reassuring me that it's not about me, it's about you and always will be. May my heart eternally beat for you and may I be ever attentive to your movements. I love you with all that I am.

In His Eyes

Introduction

This evening I stood outside in silent wonder as I gazed up at the bright full moon and the brilliant stars filling the night sky. Seeing such breathtaking beauty was a humbling reminder for me of how majestic God truly is. It also helps me remember the rich history of God's work in the world, a work I, and everyone who has ever lived or will live, is a part of. We belong to a divine story greater than ourselves. Too often, though, I become so wrapped up in the details of day-to-day living, I forget to look up and wonder at his sovereignty and mighty power. A power so great, that if we could fully see it, we would be speechlessly stunned as we fall to our knees. How miraculous then, that our God who holds the entire universe in the palm of his hand, reaches out with the same hand to touch you and me, his created treasures. This apparent paradox, that though he is sovereign and holy, he also warmly invites us into his divine presence by drawing us into his all-encompassing arms where we can enjoy his intimacy forever, is one of the greatest miracles ever known.

Sometimes when I think about this miraculous intimacy I share with God, I imagine the look in his eyes as he sees me. I imagine it is a look filled with an indescribable love, unfathomable grace, and passionate desire. However, every so often I become so ashamed of what I think of as my sinful creature-hood, that I look down away from his gaze to avoid seeing the look of reproach I think I will find there. But then he reaches out and lifts my face so I can see his love and forgiveness. He tells me I do not have to be ashamed of who I am, that he has used my struggles to reflect his glory, and that he has already done all the work necessary for reconciliation. All I have to do is to enjoy him and to rest in the peace of trusting his almighty wisdom and guidance. He then shows me a picture of the beautiful person he sees in me and the beautiful people he sees around me, encouraging me to live out of his light and not my own, a light he holds before me in the deep centrality of his eyes. There is freedom in that thought for everyone, that we all are in his hands, protected, guided, and transformed, even when we can't see it. This freedom in love then releases us to share ourselves with each other, a connectedness that is based on God's love where we can together listen for his voice spoken through the Holy Spirit.

During this time we spend in God's hands and in communion with his beloved ones, the Lord delights in opening our own eyes so we may see things we never noticed before. We begin to realize that God wants to be present in every minute aspect of our lives from when we feed the squirrels, to when we celebrate a birthday, to when we mourn the death of a loved one. He wants to dance with us whether it is a beautiful blue sky day or a stormy, rain-filled night. Through highs and lows, times of delight and times of pain, he walks with us, carries us, and speaks our name. All this is for his glory, so he may be praised throughout all the earth and the star-filled skies. This is what it means to be in his eyes: We know we are his and he is God, forever and ever and always.

Sarah Katreen Hoggatt
Salem, Oregon
November 16, 2005

Drawn to Him

Down the road I see his face,
calling out my name,
I run to him as he draws me close,
uniting in one flame.

Morning's Grace

Stars fade back into the morn
    as I rise from cloudless night,
    leave the house to tread in the field
and find the one for whom I am born.

Together in silence when dawn's light bends
    away from the world's demands,
    I reach out to touch the Lord of my heart,
my guide, my love, and my friend.

In none but him I find my rest
    while I tell him of all that hinders me
    from seeing how faithful he has been,
and the robes of beauty in which I am dressed.

His voice I hear, quiet and clear,
    assuring me ever of his love,
    that he has in store a life of hope,
a life devoid of shame and fear.

He wipes my tears and kisses my face,
    then I find the courage that I need
    to face the challenges and joy of day,
my soul renewed within his grace.

Desire:
A Tribute to Love Mysticism

Lord, I silently sit before you.
I am waiting with great desire
for you my Lover to come to me.
Come to me quickly that
I may know you intimately and long.
Come to me with fire so I
may be consumed in your passion.
Seduce me my God.
Seduce me into the blazing
flames of your holiness.
I want to know your hands upon my face,
I long to feel your kiss upon my mouth.
Hold me close unto your heart oh God,
wrap me tight into your embrace.
May I sense every movement you make,
every touch of your spirit.
May I entwine into you my very soul,
twisted together into sublime union,
experiencing you in all of your raging glory,
possessing me and transfusing everything I am.
May this be our destiny, our ever present reality,
that you will one day come and claim your bride.
Lord, let it come!

Question for God

Could you put your arms around me,
let me lay my head upon your shoulder?
Just hold me for a little while
so I know I am not here alone,
that I do not have to be the only one
carrying this burden upon my back
but that you are here to share it,
to help me walk along this way.
Let me feel your loving touch,
the warmth of your hand reaching out
to give me solace and to provide
the place of rest I'm longing for.
It is amazing how quickly your
trusted touch caresses my heart,
how healing your drawn-out hug can be.
Your tenderly given touch I crave.
Would you do it now if I asked you?
I know you could, but will you?

Drawn to Him

Heavenly Gain

My Lord and my God,
  your lover I'll be,
    ignoring the crowds
I'll listen to thee.

Although I may struggle
  to not please those around,
    I want to please you
for it is to you I am bound.

I will keep in my heart
  your ever-stayed hand,
    knowing the rest will work out
though I don't understand.

I love you dear Jesus
  and I'll trust in you,
    listening to your tender voice
to hear your words so true.

There are many other voices
  that would lead me far away,
    but I am choosing to follow you
so I'll be with you on our wedding day.

Then at that time we'll fulfill our vows,
  and you will claim your bride,
    I will live in your light forever
and you'll keep me at your side.

But right now it can be hard to see
  the reality that we'll know,
    yet I will put my hope in you
so you can help me grow.

Another Way

There's got to be
    another way.
To live, to die,
    to breathe in each day
        with God
            in every worshipful movement.
There's got to be
    a better way
        to praise him,
        to walk,
        to skip, to fly,
        to run through the meadow
            exploring
                the smallest parts
                    of his greatest trees.
Somewhere out there
    is a path
        where I can walk
        closer to him,
    a path
        I have yet to find,
somewhere beyond what
    I can now see.
But one day I will
    discover it.
One day this
    desire for God
        will be satisfied
            and I will
                follow his path
                  with joy.

Within Every Heart

There is a struggle
within every heart
to walk free.
Not freedom to bear arms
or to hold public meeting,
but to express itself
with no fear of judgment.
To know that "This is
who I am," and
be free to express it.
There is hope.
Hope that someone
would love them enough
to hold them when they cry.
To simply be with them,
to give them the comfort
they need when
hope seems far away.
There is the desire to
know of something greater
than oneself, the need
to feel wonder while
gazing up into the darkening sky.
To feel that even in
our struggle there is
"the great design" and
the Great Designer
who placed within us
all our needs that all
point to him.

In His Eyes

Draining Days

I am on my knees tonight,
my strength is flattened, taken flight.

The day's been draining and I am tired
thinking of all the things transpired.

Too many demands have left me shaking
and my mind inside is quaking.

I thought I knew the way to go
but there were things I didn't know.

How can I complete what I need to do
when I'm feeling so far from you?

For deep inside of me I crave
your presence beside me, your hand to save.

There is nothing here in my life I want more
than to feel your spirit pour

into my soul as you share in my tears,
as you let me know you're carrying me here.

Though the day be exhausting and long,
I cling to you for you are my song,

my hope, my joy, the one I adore,
and the one I will hold to forevermore.

Come Away

Come away my beloved
into the secret recesses
of myself where your soul
will be smoothed
beneath the ministrations
of my soothing hand
and your hot tears
will be swept away in
the cool light within my
penetrating gaze of tenderness.
Let me take you far above
into my realm of consolation
and redemption.
I will show you who you are,
the delight you are to me
and the glory I created you for.
Leave the cares of this
world behind and do not
be afraid of them,
for I am greater than they.
They will soon pass away
but I– I remain the same.
I want to help you,
to comfort you,
to bring you into myself.
But first I need you to
let go of what you think
is irrefutable,
of what you consider to be solid.
I need you to empty your hands
so I can fill them.
So come away with me my beloved.
Come away, come away.

Spiritual Direction

Journeying along eternity's shore,
wrapped in the presence of the Holy Spirit,
there is a companion to point out what I do not see,
someone to help discern the movements of God
in the ever abounding waves of my being.
To find the flow of God in the seasons of my life,
teaching me how to be, simply be and not do.
What a gift to have a warm hand to hold
while together we find the threads of hope
woven through the clouds.
To have someone
with whom I can share my questions,
my weeping, my quintessential self.
Someone who has seen my pain,
with whom I don't have to
fill up the quiet with words,
but who helps me discern where I am
with the lover of my soul.
Finding God in meaningful silence,
this divine connection
nourishing the care of my spirit,
giving me a quiet joy and comforting peace.
A fellow traveler who sits beside me when it rains,
drinking deeply when I need to lose myself,
holding up God's light in the darkness
so I can find myself in his presence once again.
This guide who assures me I do not walk alone
toward the throne room of God.

On Retreat

God, you ask me
why I came here
and although you know
the answer, perhaps
you wanted me to
clarify it for myself.
I wanted to be
somewhere where the
only thing asked of me
was to be with you,
where living consists of
hearing the birds sing,
breathing in the
majestic smell of the pines,
and being awed by the
beauty set before me.
I came to regain a
sense of who you are
without any of my interpretations.
To restore my view of forever
and to reclaim the
promises you have
sacrificed to give me.
Lord, I have come to seek your face
and to lay myself before your feet.
So now that I have come
and given answer to your question,
please speak to one of mine.
Why have you brought me here?
What words do you
want me to hear?
What warmth of your presence
shall I carry forth in my heart?
I need your guidance,

In His Eyes

your everlasting presence.
I have to be where you are
and I will seek the ends
of the mountains to find you.
Perhaps that is why we came—
to seek each other
in the silence.

Drawn to Him

Center Down

When your heart
feels flustered,
stressed and overdone,
close your eyes
and stop your steps
looking to the One
who is there to calm you
out on the woeful sea,
who is always
there to talk with you
throughout eternity.
The only peace you'll
ever find
only comes from him,

and the only one who
will ever know and
forgive your deepest sin,
whispers that he loves you
every time you come to him.
So when your heart
feels tired
and inside you wear a frown,
find yourself in the one
who's there,
look up
and center down.

In His Eyes

Shaddai

You fill me up and leave
      me wanting more.
You take me into your arms even as
      I am left reaching for them.
Shaddai, you let me hear your voice,
      I turn my head and I long to hear it again.
Where are you my God?
      Where can I find you?
Is there a place where I can feel
      your breath beside me?
Is there somewhere, anywhere,
      where I can touch you?
The more I know you,
      the more I crave you.
The more I see you, it seems
      the less I comprehend you.
Yet the longer I yearn to gaze
      upon your glorious face,
the more you show yourself to me
      and the deeper I am in love with you.

The Quest

I am on a quest
to find the love of God.
Perhaps if I run through the corn field,
I will find him among the bountiful harvest
and know I am cared for.
But no, I am hungry
and my heart is tired.
Maybe if I sink below the water's waves,
I will see him in the
mysterious depths
of a world I know not
and I could comprehend great things.
Nay, for I would sink and drown
without him to hold to
having only a human understanding.
What if I sought him out
among the desert mothers?
I could wander through the wilderness
and ask their advice
then know I have found the way,
the white way.
But looking around at the world,
I realize there is no black and white,
the world is filled with fantastic colors
raising their radiance to the sky.
So where do I find him, what can I do?
There is nothing I can do...
All I can do is be...
be a seeker of his heart, of his love—
then to know I always had his love
no matter where I went in search for it,
he was always there pouring himself out upon me.
Extraordinary...
all this time he too was on a quest... for me.

In His Eyes

Growing Through the Struggle

Compost can be hard to take
as it pours out what we don't know,
but when laid out upon our lives
it gives us the nutrients to grow.

Teach

Teach, you say.
Teach what?
What do I know that is worthy of being heard?
What is worth taking from my
introspective heart and giving to the world?
What you have taught me?
I can't imagine what that could be.
I mean, yes, you have shown me things
I have never seen before and given me
understanding of things I could never comprehend.
But what could you possibly want
with a servant such as me?
There are so many wiser people out there
and they can reach a much wider audience than I.
Teach. But you are choosing me?
I am young Lord, with so much to learn myself.
How could you do this thing?
Sometimes I feel so inadequate for the tasks
you have already given to me,
let alone the task you're asking.
How can you know how I feel?
You've been there too? Yes, I suppose you were.
My pain? What does my own anguish
have to do with any of this?
Out of my greatest pain
will come my greatest ministry?
What in the heck is that supposed to mean?
We are best able to teach what we
have first become acquainted with?
What have I become acquainted with God?
Your might in my darkness?
Oh, well yes, I suppose that's true.
And yes, I do hear your voice.
You are the best of my life.

Teach.
But God, you have heard me speak.
I am not good with the spoken word,
I trip over what to say.
It's like walking across marbles on the floor
and more times than I enjoy admitting,
my face has become much better acquainted
with the ground below and I want to hide from you
and from everyone else in fervent humiliation.
So you see Lord why I cannot teach.
I am simply not made for it.
Who am I to say what I am made for?
Do I feel the burning fire you have put into my heart?
Truth? Yes.
Yes, I've sensed your words of fiery wisdom, deeper than I.
Why do you look at me like that?
God, I just…I mean…God, why?
Why this thing, why teach them what I hear and know?
I'm just supposed to trust you?
To walk out into thin air with no fear…
Yeah, that sounds like fun.
Then again,
could it indeed be that I have something to say?
Is it possible out of all the impossible
possibilities I have something of substance
to teach, to give to those who will listen?
You have done amazing things before Lord.
Could this be one of your miracles in me?
I have your tools in my hands and your voice
speaking in my mind, is it really
your utterance, your shape of expression?
Teach.
I am but your bowed servant, and yet
you touch your burning coal to my mouth
and say, "Go, speak my word."
Okay, Lord. I will teach your heart.

Living the Question

There are many questions in my mind
        as my answers before unwind.
I wonder if I ever really had
        my feet on ground, or was it bad?
Was what I had ever true?
        Was there ever any shadow of you?

The world is rolling beneath my feet
        as I'm feeling my fearful heart beat.
Who am I now supposed to trust?
        What is righteous? Who is just?
Will I ever find what I seek?
        Will my voice ever find the freedom to speak

of what my heart is longing to feel
        and how my mind is crying to heal?
But perhaps I could not live them now,
        the answers I seek as I bow and ask how.
Living the questions may be what I need,
        following God as he faithfully leads.

Though I have already come a long way,
        I lift my heart up to God to pray
so I might see from where he is,
        to know that I am always his.
For even though these questions assail,
        I know who holds the answers still.

So now I will walk along his side
        and in his glory forever abide.

Ode to Shame

Sometimes do you feel like running
from who you are inside?
Do you ever want to do away
    with the ever crashing tide?

Would you ever like to stop the rain
from falling down at night?
Do you ever stop to take a look
    and stand cringing at the sight?

Are you familiar with the times
when you don't know what to say
because you are so ashamed
    of what has happened here today?

You wish you did not have to look
deep into their eyes,
yet you want to share with them what's real
    instead of telling lies

that you are fine just as you are,
that nothing else is wrong,
but in reality you know you're hurt
    and the battle has been long.

Too often you are holding too many things within
because of what you fear,
that they will no longer want you
    close beside them here.

But until you learn that they will love
beyond what you can do,
you will always be ashamed
    and want to run away from you.

In His Eyes

River of Tears

Split apart and alone,
      standing on either side
of a river of tears.
      Feeling abandoned and ignored,
each bypassing the boat to
      cross over to the
bank of reconciliation.
      They wonder how it happened.
For what reason was the river
      formed between them?
For what purpose
      does the water flow?
How could it have gone so wrong?
      Will they ever find each other?
Will they ever cross
      the river of tears?

Growing Through the Struggle

Swimmer's Rapids

Standing shaking on the shore,
hearing the angry water's roar,
deep green rapids before my feet
as my pain today I meet.
Fearing I will drown
if the water pulls me down,
I am terrified to see
where the torrents might take me.
How will I know where I am
if against the rocks I slam
and could I ever find my way
if the demons carry me away?
But there is no other road to take
than the one that pain will make,
so I take a breath and jump weeping in,
over my head in the realities of sin.
Surrounded by murky tears of loss
as my body thrown and tossed,
pulled at by those who would rip me apart,
Satan ready to kill my heart.
I fight against the waves for air
when I feel the Holy Spirit there.
He buoys me up upon his strength
and gives me might to swim the length
where I am free to be in the pain,
to fully see the horror plain.
He tells me when to take a breath,
the bottom pits of the valley of death.
Then plunged down by the raging flood
the force of the water washing the blood,
pounded into the wave,
my body enslaved,
at the mercy of where the current goes,
pushed into the spray, under the flows.

Then through the midst of my desperate gasps,
I hear his voice yelling out to "Swim fast,
make for the shore
and when you can't swim anymore,
I'll throw you a rope,
I'll shine for you the light of hope."
With all my might I stroke through the river,
the effort making my tired arms quiver,
and when he sees that I'm fighting for life,
he tosses his rope bag into my strife.
I grasp the life cord into my hands
and turn my back to where he stands
so he can pull me through the deep,
through the water as it sweeps,
and as I reach him, he pulls me out
dripping wet, no longer with doubt.
For looking down, I see what he's done,
that he has finished what he'd begun.
Because of the rapids I had been through,
I looked in his eyes and saw me created anew.

The Unknown Word

How can the inexpressible
        pain be expressed?
How can the untouchable
        truth be touched?
What does the wordsmith do
        when words fail?
What action can be taken
        when every thing to be said
cannot be said?
        Where do you go?
Where do you go?

Winter's Chill

Fallen to the ground,
frozen snow beneath my feet,
I gaze up from where I lay
to see the steady sleet
of hail and wind
grey in winter's chill,
wakened without knowing,
body worn and still.
Beyond all sense of feeling,
past the point of fear,
stranger to all perceptions
as the shadow's drawing near
to take my hand in silence,
view the frost upon my face,
to stand sentry in my numbness
and give the sleep of grace.

In His Eyes

The Last Mark

God, I've missed you in the darkness,
     missed your trembling power
       as I stand here alone and shaking
       in this the final hour.
Your presence seems so far away
     and I can't hear your voice,
       I desperately need your guidance
       as I face this awful choice.
The pain seems overwhelming,
     which one do I choose?
       How can I possibly decide my mind
       when it seems either way I lose?

Who Am I?

Who am I to say
you cannot use me?
Who am I to say
I've got nothing to give?
Who am I to stand
before my Creator
and insult the one he made?
Who am I?

Wordless Night

"I have so many questions Lord,
so many things to talk over with you.
And as I come to you
in the dark of night
when the world is as still
as a leopard in her lair,
I lie beneath the covers,
reaching out to touch your hand
  that you might still my trembling soul."

Wordlessly you whisper, "I am here.
My beloved, I am here with you.
Lay upon my breast what is
burdensome to your concealed self.
I did not create you to bear this.
Let me be your refuge, your place of solace.
I will listen to you and answer you.
In the dark you will find me and
  I will still your trembling soul."

"But Lord, I cannot find the words,
I cannot select the rocks out of the stream
to line up upon the shore."
"My treasure, together we will go out
and look at them exactly where they lay.
You do not have to present them before me,
you just have to show me where they are."
"Then guide me, Lord, to the ones you most
  want to see as you still my trembling soul."

Churning Waters

Churning waters of the dark sea
push against my shivering body
trying to pull me away from the
torn tree to which I cling.
Rain lashes against my face while
the gale drowns out my frightened screams
into its convulsive, shattering roar.
If I let go, where would the ocean throw me?
Would I be lost out to sea never to return,
or would the waves wash me upon hope's shore?
Whichever I choose,
torn tree or raging sea,
the rain

        pours

             down.

Push Harder

I am angry at you.
I want to scream
and pound my fists
against you, to
jump, stomp, and kick.
To step on your feet
yelling out all my pain,
shout my accusations of why?
Vomiting up my shame,
it's your fault, you deal with it!
You're supposed to be in charge!
Why am I feeling this way God?
Can't you just let me go from this
so I don't have to feel anymore?
I'm tired of this struggle.
I even feel deeply ashamed
for yelling at you God,
an ungrateful, worthless rebel of a soul
who dares to go against you.
For even though I want to be
passionately after your heart,
I am raw and cower at the mountain,
weary of fighting my way through.
I want to go at you in a boxing ring,
to get in as many punches as I can
before you knock me unconscious
for such revolting behavior.
I wouldn't blame you for that God, because
even while I am telling you off,
I shake with remorse,
        yet I'm scared
        and I don't know what else to do.

God at My Bedside

Like the prodigal son I have wandered.
Needing untold answers to endless questions,
I have tread through foreign lands eating the sand.
My mouth is dry and my courage is at an ebb.
Down to the core of myself,
through the storms of night
I have wrestled with the angels,
cut and broken I have struggled with all my might.
Then by the grace of God I collapsed and was
blind folded, my hands were bound.
Passed from one to the next,
disoriented and frightened,
I wondered where I was and
whose were the hands that moved me.
It was then I gave up,
utterly spent and poured out upon the earth.
My heart lost consciousness, I knew no more.
Trusting in you Lord that you would
carry and keep a hold of me
when I couldn't hold myself,
trust enveloped my being and
I relied on what I could not see and touch.
Unable to walk, or speak, or do anything for myself,
I felt entirely taken up into your loving hands.
A strange and quiet joy permeated the air in
my world of disconnectedness
and I came to be at peace in the midst of numbness.
Now, yet blinded, I lie in a room
dazed in a raging fever.
I can feel your hand bathing my face
as you sit at my bedside
humming a lullaby.
You nourish me with your words
and when I drift off again into delusion,

you are yet there, holding my lifeless hands in yours.
Sometimes I think I hear you cry for your child;
you cry the tears I do not know how to cry.
You pray the prayers I do not know how to pray.
When I wake you tell me stories,
you tell me how this is a good place
and I believe you.
Through the fog of pain I see your eyes,
and when I drift off once more,
your face is the last thing I see.

Eye of the Storm

Standing in the eye of the storm,
I ask you not to take me
out of the raging winds,
but to calm my fears within them.
To just be present to the experience
in the midst of the rolling thunder
and avalanche of beating rain.
Help me to let the
gale force me where it will.
I am in your hands.
I will drink this cup of fury;
let it cleanse me from
all that is not right
before your presence.
I pray you give me the strength
to see you in the storm,
to lift up my head, and sing.

In His Eyes

Pilate

Eyes of calm while
mine are in the fire.
Confusion are my thoughts,
sweaty are my hands.
As firm as stone he stands,
like a statue of Caesar
unmoved.
This, the Son of God?
Thorns for gold,
blood for kisses,
how could this be?
A king, an innocent king.
Shouts pound in,
the people scream.
The people want him crucified.
I, with threats of treason,
falling to the flames.
I lift my hands for water
as the nails fall.

Before the Mountain

"Oh God of my soul,
I feel as if I have let you down,
as if what you believed me
capable of is in fact, not true.
Forgive my weakness Father,
I don't seem able to do this thing."
"What do you think you have done wrong?"
"I have failed you and
humiliated myself."
"You have not failed me.
You are learning and that takes time.

Give yourself the grace of mistakes,
you will get better."

      "But God, what I want to do and
      what I do, do not seem to be connected.
      How can that change?"

"The mountain always seems
insurmountable when seen from the valley.
But on your way up, gradually,
it becomes easier, even enjoyable.
Then when you reach the top
you will look down
and see how far you have come.
I promise you, your feet will find
sure footing."

      "But Lord, what if I fall down a cliff
      or lose my balance on the precipice?"

"Then I will be there to catch you
and set you right again."

      "It seems so hard Lord..."

"I know, but it starts with
just one step, and you are
determined to make it up
to the top, are you not?"

      "You know I am, but I fear it too."

"Yes, I feel your fear, but you have
nothing to be afraid of.
I'm the only one watching you
and you know what I'm doing?"

      "What are you doing Lord?"

"I'm cheering."

My Grandpa's Voice

I heard it in the early morning
waking up to Grandpa's mush,
his duct taped slippers
padding along the cold linoleum
of the trailer floor.
His eyes, my eyes, greet me
as I happily scramble into his lap,
legs dangling over the side,
leaning my head to listen to the
rhythmic cadences of his heart beat.

I heard his laughter reverberate
in the cab as he took "his girls"
on a joy ride in his new
truck through the countryside.
Jumping over fire pits like Tinkerbelle,
I hear him call to my mom
for a band-aid and then object when
they rush him to the hospital for stitches.
And me, always running back for that
second hug and "I love you."

Then quietly I listened to his voice
as he stuttered his words
in the late afternoon
but when he curses in
frustration they are quite clear.
Pictures on the wall
show visits too infrequent
and a beloved cat named Willy,
desperately missed.
What he would give for a beer.

Now I cannot hear his voice over the
screaming in my own head and his
coughs as he drowns in his lungs.
His only word is "Help" and the severest word
of ultimate goodbye I am required to give
cannot form itself under the boulders of my tears.
I hold his hand in mine, a life vest against reality
of these priceless moments before the gate of death.
Then when the dreaded moment has come to be
and I have uttered the black words of loss,
I sink to the floor
knowing I will hear his voice no more.

In His Eyes

Transformations

The broken colored shards of our spirits
God transforms to be
windows shining forth his light,
his glory for all to see.

Ransomed Rose

God, when I think I cannot do it,
I look at you and see
a man who struggled to see it through
as you were dying on that tree.
Fighting underneath the weight
that this task will be too much,
I gaze upon your praying hands
and the soldier's bloody touch.
And when I wonder if indeed
I am the one you chose,
you look out from the grave you left
and call your ransomed rose.

Behold Your Freedom

When God gazes down upon us,
        he doesn't see what we can do,
he sees the souls that he created,
        the souls remade anew.

He understands that we will sin
        when we try for him and fail,
and he'll be there to pick us up
        as we experience life and quail.

The freedom that he died to give
        lets us be just who we are,
a faithful people with humbled hearts
        guided by his stars.

We may not be the uppity
        people of the land,
but we will see his glory
        and we'll behold his mighty hands

that have guided us all through our lives,
        low though they may be,
but the first is last and the last is first
        when we reach eternity.

The Poet's Dilemma

Each day
      another word,
      another masterpiece
      to fix upon the sky.
A way of knowing,
      of being,
      of discerning the
      world anew.
To watch, to wait,
      to grapple with the
      unknown fragments
      hiding in the haze.
Guided by temperance,
      instructed through time,
      I raise my head,
      put down my pen,
and breathe in
      the sun's rebirth.

Silence

Reposed in the silence my soul is stilled.
All is quiet as I let go of the nonessential
and find the space between thoughts where
my spirit finds the freedom to breathe.
A place where I can notice
all the things I usually pass by,
to travel light when things grow faint,
and to sigh and weep all the deep-felt emotions
words can never hope to tell.
In the cool of evening when silence is grown,
God whispers wonders to the hushed hearts
of those who know the fullness of absence,
to those who stop to hear
what the heart is free to feel
and whose eyes draw into the depths of inaudibility
to see themselves as they truly are,
and to know in the stillness, who they are to God.

Gift of Tears

Bowing down while seeking the gift of tears,
I wrestle with the floods held back behind the dam.
I ask you to help me to
stop to lament what I have lost—
to pause to express the release I have gained.
Let the ache in my heart assist me in
finding the freedom to sink down below the surface of
cautiousness into the depths of emotional inaudibility,
and please heal the broken fragments in my hands
as I hold them out to you in mute anguish.
For I know that by my tears I shall be cleansed
and through my tears I shall be made whole.

In His Eyes

Study of a Portrait

Face to face, looking
    at a picture with no glass,
        it's just you and the canvas
           staring at each other,
                searching for what each one is.
Nothing to hide behind,
    the only light reflected
        is the warmth the creator instilled.
           There is no protective layer to polish,
                no barrier to see through.
Colors vibrantly run
    forth before your eyes
        as you reach out to touch
           the lumps of paint
                dried from when they fell.
Transfixed by the artist's revelation
    of terrible truth and startling beauty,
        the image haunts you
           and silently shows you what is,
              who you are, and the
                countless possibilities of
              what could be.

Seasons

Burnt leaves floating to the ground,
a graceful letting go of the life that was
as we grieve for what has gone yet
anticipate what is still to come.
We enjoy each season for the gift it is,
each one bringing new sights and
ever deepening realizations and points of view.
How else can we enjoy a world
captured in white crystal silence
permeated in a peace that pervades our hearts
or rejoice as we slide along a frozen river?
As one season passes another,
we learn old things at new heights,
revisiting old themes with new twists.
Holding onto what we know, then
watching it unfold like the first roses of March,
their sweet fragrance welcoming us
to see with new eyes the earth's rebirth.
Gardens are planted as daffodils sing
and robins return to revel in spring.
Our lives are constantly moving through
seasons and if we look back too long at one long past
or anxiously await one that has yet to arrive,
we will miss the one that is.
We will not see the blue lake
longing to envelope us in its depth
below the sweltering sun
or wonder upon the fireworks bursting in the sky.
The glorious riches of blackberries
and the glow of warm campfires
will be lost to us if we
do not take the hour to enjoy them.
And though we may have seen
this season many moons ago,

In His Eyes

it is different every time.
Each time is unique and precious,
just like the Artist's leaves
we launch ourselves into once again.

Vision

I will not be deterred,
my heart will not be dissuaded.
This choice I have made,
this laying down of
what I have thus far known
and the taking up of
what I believe can be
is the journey set
before my feet.
The line drawn,
the curtain parted.
I will try,
I will see it through.
And if I fail,
     at least I have
         dared–
            and lived.

In the Silence of the Night

In the silence of the night
beneath the moon below,
in a field alit with silver
and lightning bugs aglow,
I fell asleep among the stars
created long ago.

I wandered among the clouds
and danced along the stream,
I skipped the stones into the pools
where living mercies teamed.
Then in the fog I saw you...
far and veiled you seemed.

In His Eyes

I took a few steps forward
to see your beauty fair,
I then held back in trembling fear–
I'd gone as far as I would dare.
I saw how nak'd I was before you
so hid in darkness bare.

The breeze so cool moved through the wood,
the leaves rustl'd overhead,
you looked to where I was hiding,
you looked to where I had tread,
then gently upon the ground you knelt
and prayed to Heav'n overhead.

The look I saw within your eyes
brought tears upon my face,
the love I saw upon your hands
spoke of tenderness and grace.
Yet still I quivered to come to you
for you were regal in this place.

Though quiet you looked mighty
as you gazed again my way,
and though I knew just what I was,
I could no longer stay
behind the tree of shame and guilt
away from where you lay.

Weeping I came before you,
afraid of what you'd do,
would you turn me far away,
a world away from you
where I could no longer hear your voice
or be in constant view?

But before I could get to where you were,
you had me in your arms,
and before I could confess just one small thing
you had me wrapped within your charms
of your love so bold while mercy rolled
over all my doubts disarmed.

You told me I was precious
and perfect in your eyes,
that you had already paid the price
for all my sin, demeaned-filled lies,
and that we were bound together
through all the lows and mountain highs.

Then you took my hands into your own,
wiped away my tears,
tied purple ribbons in my hair
to chase away the fears,
then leaned down to whisper in my ear
what I've only longed to hear.

The echoed melody of your voice
changed the light before my eyes,
and the sounds ringing in my ears
hushed my anxious cries.
"I am ever here surrounding you,
nothing can break these ties."

Now I stand before you
dressed in garments new,
a fresh reality in my heart,
a freedom I never knew.
For now I know my own great worth
because I am loved by you.

Beat of Change

Change invariably comes,
>   altering the regular beats
>   of our lives into a
>   strange new melody.
Whether it tumbles in
>   as rocks down a hill
>   shattering into unrecognizable
>   shards all we once knew,
or as the tinkling of bells
>   reminding us of something
>   beyond ourselves,
>   change makes itself known
in between the crevices
>   and in the shadows of corners,
>   hiding behind an illusioned
>   world of predictability we have
laid deep within our lives.
>   We wonder at it,
>   try to understand its way,
>   but how can you understand something
that is always remaking itself?
>   Are we even meant to comprehend the
>   chords of change and the turning
>   of movements sung through
the strings of our hope and pain?
>   Or is there indeed divine
>   guidance within them?
>   Surely change will come,
but the question is...
>   how will you respond to it?
>   What note will you play
>   in the song of change?

X is for Xylophone

When you are young,
they tell you x is for xylophone,
Santa Claus is jolly,
and stories will always end
happily ever after.
But now I know that
x can also stand for x-ray,
pictures of pain.
I also know those cookies
so eagerly set out on Christmas Eve
by naughty and nice little hands
are annually eaten by groggy parents
up too late and awake too early,
and that those stories don't always
have a happy ending.
Sometimes Red Riding Hood gets eaten
and the prince doesn't always stay.
Yet, after all these years,
I still remember
x is for xylophone.

Caterpillar-Goo

Caterpillars weaving their cocoons
as if they know it's time to change,
time to be transformed.
Curled up in winter's rest,
their structure is taken apart
as the creature is content
to be caterpillar-goo for a time,
for they know when the sun
shines brightly once again,
they will emerge from their
encapsulated rooms
to spread their wings
and show the Creator's glory.

In His Eyes

Learning to Trust His Love

Learning to trust his bridge of love
as we see the passion in his eyes,
we take the step of faith in him
and feel our spirits rise.

Creation's Song

Once there was the Word
who lived upon the sea,
but he was all alone
and longed to hearken thee.

He sailed upon vast waters
and played upon the air,
floated on the ocean tide
with seemingly no care.

But each morning was eternity,
each night was dark and cold,
there was no one to share it with,
no loving hand to hold.

Then one day he took a look
and knew what he must do.
He said, "I'll take out of all I am
and create something for you."

"Oh, I'll create it beautiful
and take your breath away.
You will stand amazed at this
at the dawning of the day.

You'll revel in the colors
and the brightness of the sun.
Then you'll turn to me
and wonder at all that I have done.

We will be so happy,
together you and I,
you will be mine forever
even after when you die.

For I will give you part of me,
my light will shine from you.
I will live within your heart,
this I promise I will do.

But so you will not be forced to come
upon this journey here,
I will give you the choice between
my laughter and your tears.

Though some of you will turn away
never to come back home,
many of you will return again,
never more to roam.

I will be there with you
and carry you along the way.
I will pay the price for you
of when you go astray.

I will take the nails
in my hands and in my feet,
and it will be my side they pierce,
my body they will beat.

It will be my crown of thorns
they place upon my brow
and it will be my shoulders
of whom the cross is given now.

I will bear the mockers
and I will shed the blood,
and I will be the one
to whom they throw the mud.

In His Eyes

I promise to you that I will be
the one who shouts out 'God,
why have you forsaken me
and taken away your rod?'

Then I will be the one
to bow my head and die,
and I will be the one
to utter the sinful cry.

You see, I would rather die
and forever be with you,
than spend eternity all alone
and never death go through.

But you are my beloved child
of whom I love to sing,
and knowing always is what we have
makes me feel just like a king.

You will never know the pain
of what your sins demand,
for I will have already paid the price
and smited death's dark hand.

You will see the glory of it all
because I will rise again,
and you will rise beside me,
what rejoicing we'll have then!

For death can never hold
the God who created all,
the Father God who wakes the morn
inside of Heaven's halls.

My protective hand will hold you,
there will be no fear,
I will fight your battles
and put my angels near.

Then when it's time for you to die,
I'll receive you in my arms,
you will see me face-to-face
and we'll dance among the stars.

But right now there is only blackness,
a blank and empty night.
I wonder what I should bring forth first?
I know, I will start with light."

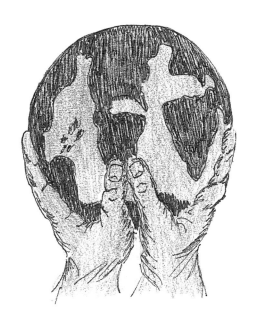

A Plea for Peace Within

I know in my mind I'll be alright
because my God has said
      that he is watching out for me,
knows the hairs upon my head.
But the problem is to tell my heart,
it doesn't understand.
      It thinks of many things unknown
and doesn't see his hand.

But if the lilies of the valley
are dressed beyond compare–
      why should I be worried,
why hold onto what I bear?
For worries become so heavy
like rocks I trudge around,
      hiding them from the ones I love
while their ties around me bound.

Everything will be set to right,
God works it out for good.
      Even though I don't see it now,
it comes out as it always should.
So I will now trust in what he says,
I'll try not to fear,
      for he is guiding every step
and gives me peace while I am here.

Guided on Your Trail

Take this hand
and let it move across the page
guided by your voice.
Help me not to hinder, or to judge,
but to let you be
the awesome presence that you are.
Help me to step in synch with you,
walking by your glory,
running in the expanse of your grace.
Pray, move my thoughts
along your trails of wonder
where you want them to go
then let me dwell there with you.
Speak through me, Lord.
You say you are the Word,
let me be yours.

In His Eyes

Lift Up Thine Eyes

When I'm alone
and want to know
you're near,
I step into the vast expanse
of soaring black velvet
and look to the stars.
The silvery orb
that shines above
has shone upon you too,
and perhaps while
I am wondering
at the sparklers in the sky,
you're standing beside me
looking to the
heavens on high.
In this world
where things are
sometimes too good to be true
and people are not always what they seem,
I need a reminder that you're real
and ever present here.
So I lift up my eyes
and look to the stars.

Seeing Jesus for the First Time

What a wonder,
what sweet grace,
to see the joy within your eyes
          and the smile upon your face.
One of my greatest dreams
has now become to be
a living, breathing person here
          walking alongside me.
I look at you
and hardly trust my eyes,
because you are what I needed,
          the answer to all my cries.
Let me revel in this light
and enjoy this dream come true,
the love I've found within your heart
          and the delight I know with you.

Could This Be?

Could this be that I may let
my appropriateness go,
to come out from under the sheets of shame
into a world of grace where my
voice is free to flow?
Could this be that I now have the freedom
to paint my life in sweeping colors
on a broad canvas beautiful and new,
stretched across the sea of time?
Can this be? Can this be?
By his blood, I believe this can be.

In His Eyes

Falling Up

When I hear your whispered words
upon the cool night air,
I close my eyes and brush your face
to feel your love so fair.
The beauty of the evening
is reflected in your eyes,
and the brilliance of the stars
are straight from Heaven's skies.
Say those words again to me,
the ones I long to hear,
that you have loved me enough to die
just so I'd be near.
Sing to me the song of grace
created long ago,
then I will look into your heart
and see the moon below.

Doctor God

I know you're here beside my bed
watching over me as I sleep.
I can hear you singing songs of love
as my hands in yours you keep.

I can feel your touch upon my skin
as you gently bathe my brow,
and I can feel you lift me up
as from place to place you move me now.

Though I'm weak and cannot stand,
although I know I'm ill,
I sense we're in a miracle
for you do wonders still.

Who I am is changing
while I lie within your arms,
for you've become the breath I breathe
and your voice the healing balm.

Now so still I lie here,
my eyes gazing upon your face,
you hold me close against your chest,
awashed in healing grace.

Take Me Out to the Ballgame

Once again, you did not choose me.
Once again, I am the last one picked of
all the options to have within your life
like the last one selected for a team,
the one with hunched shoulders in the dirt all alone.
You hate to be rejected, cast aside.
So do I. I abhor being the one you turn to last,
the God in your pocket of last resorts.
Could this day be the day you look to me
and say I want you to go up to bat for me?
Could this be the one when you
let me coach the game?
Let this be the inning you invite me
to run upon your playing field,
yelling and screaming, cheering you on.
Let me just hear you say my name.
I am right here, choose me!
I cannot fail to bring you home—
and when we win,
I will carry you on my shoulders in
redemptive triumph!

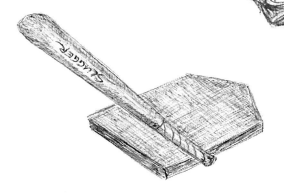

River Guide

Through the swirling waters
    I hear my Father's voice,
    he tells me of his love and grace
    and of his eternal choice.

He is the one who guides me
    upon life's river way,
    and he is the one whose laughter I hear
    at the close of every day.

I pray the Lord will teach me
    how to obey his grand commands,
    as we are rafting through the rapids
    then landing safely on the sands.

In His Eyes

Mercy Speaks

My Lord and my Father,
I trudge with heavy heart
to you this night for
my beloved one is grieving,
their anguish as a fire
burning myself within.
Rather would it be I
treading in the flames,
the orange light
reflected in my eyes.
Let it be my own two feet
searing with aching agony
as I tread the scorching coals.
Let it be my flesh that takes the pain.
Let it be my heart that fills with their sorrow.
I would rather it be me who knows
the despair of sinful consequence
rather than watch them suffer
unendurable shame down where
I cannot reach them.
For I love them more than
the very breath I breathe,
more than the blood that flows
through the veins in my hands.
As long as they are safe in my arms,
falling into death is a
price I will gladly pay.

Is There an End?

I asked the Lord, "Is there an end
    to the blessings you have given?"
And he said, "No, my child.
    This was made in Heaven.
This is a gift that's always
    sure and true.

This delight designed
    specifically for you.
You see, there's a greater love
    beyond what you can see—
and you will have it for
    all eternity.

You are my forever treasure
    and I enjoy to give
blessings to thrill your heart,
    gifts to remind you that I live.
So when you fear they won't be there,
    these gifts you've come to know,

understand I will not give
    then reverse the flow.
Even if these blessings pass
    away from your life's sight,
know I am bringing greater
    gifts from Heaven's light."

In His Eyes

Guided by Wisdom

We are tall ships upon the sea
guided by his light,
as he teaches us his wisdom
upon life's ocean bright.

One Day I Sat With the Wise...

...And asked what greatness is.
For it seemed to me the world
was full of people well known,
full of talents and gifts,
beautiful of face and
riches beyond compare.
Surely, this is what greatness is.
The wise sat in silence
and looked out to the sea,
looked at my face and said,
"This is what greatness is.
It's when you have fallen
and get up again.
When you give everything
you have when nothing is left.
It's crying all your tears
then finding a smile.
To go on when you
want to go home.
It's following what you believe
instead of what others claim,
to dare to think—and follow through.
Greatness is to stand alone
yet being courageous enough
to stand united together.
It's to see the vision beyond
what you know and
to realize there is more
beyond what is you.
Greatness is walking through the fire
when you could have taken a swim,
to do what is right and
not what is acceptable.
Greatness is to seek God's face

Guided by Wisdom   73

in the darkness and when
you find it, to let all other lesser things go
and to hold onto him with your entire self.
That's what greatness is."

Trust the Unseen

Through the fog of morning dawn
as it blinds your way,
not able to see what you walk towards–
lost out in the grey.
Shapes have lost their shadows,
tears fall from eyes unseen,
groping around for what you seek–
the dream of sunlight's gleam.
Though you may be stumbling,
hear his voice call you at your side,
for there is danger in the shadows
and now you must decide.
Though the way may seem confused,
to him it's light as day,
trust his unseen guidance
though you feel lost out in the grey.

In His Eyes

The Road of Two Seas

The road of two seas
     is a hard one to tread,
     for on one is sweet terror
and on the other you're dead.

The path between is narrow
     and slippery at best,
     so one will need to choose
to pass eternity's test.

Which of the seas is safer
     for a human soul?
     Which of them holds life within
and the power to make us whole?

Do not be deceived
     by what seems to be,
     for neither one
can be what you foresee.

One sea seems calm,
     controllable and safe.
     The waves gently lap
upon the shore of your belief.

But beneath the crystal green
     is hidden a soul in need.
     Knowing no full expression,
it is left to bleed.

The other sea is stormy
     and difficult to view.
     The rocks below lets no one know
what lies beyond the blue.

Yet this is the sea to enter in
     for in it you will grow,
     challenged by our God on high,
you will be amazed at where you go.

So choose the one
     holding faith and flame,
     for within it the dawn will come
and you'll never be the same.

The other may look kinder
     but kindness is held within,
     the outside is only gilding
hiding fear and sin.

Ask the Lord to guide you
     as you make this eternal choice.
     Fear or faith within your heart,
pride or love to voice.

Keep Christ's face before you,
     pray on humbled knees,
     his wisdom will help guide you
as you walk the road of seas.

In His Eyes

Sacrifice

It is easy to give
up your life when you
have little to live for,
little to lose,
but would you still
give it up when the
delights in your life
outnumber the sorrows?
Would you still be willing
to let it go
when you want
to hold on?

Kicking Complacency

We have become a complacent people,
too content with taking the easy way
and prepackaged avenue of gluttony
and all-you-can-buy indulgences,
never caring what will come.
We are so busy thinking of
what we can take from someone,
we don't give heed to the life-giving
rivers of human kindness we can pour
out into the dry riverbeds of hurting souls.
We may come and we may go,
but I wonder if our hearts
were ever really there?
Have we chosen to slander the truth?
Have we forgotten that with great power

comes great responsibility?
Yet it is not about us, it never was.
We serve one greater than ourselves.
By his strength we can do much more
than what we have done.
I believe this.
Do you?

Humbled Before Him

If I could speak with wisdom
and tell all that you should know,
would I be great and wonderful
by putting on a theist show?
If I could move with stately grace
exquisite as a dove,
would my reward be greater
in the kingdom up above?
If I lived a blameless life
and every choice was right,
would God love me more than all the rest,
would I be special in his sight?
But no matter what we do down here,
we are humbled before his throne.
We all have fallen short of him
and deserve punishment unknown.
But because he has chosen to take our place,
to be the sinner slain,
we will be raised to life with him,
forever with him we will reign.
Though we are imperfect,
we are cleansed by loving tears,
and he will take us to him
even yet while we are here.

Generational Sins

Somewhere in the eaves it began,
high up in the cobwebs–
made by spiders long gone.
Betwixt the dust and the nails,
devouring the darkness,
darkening the light,
it slumber—ever growing colder.
Down through the depths it ever moves–
building one upon another.
Unseen, invariably felt.
Creeping through the walls,
it wafts throughout the rooms,
poisoning all those who stay
and never leave.

Judgment Be Still

Where do you dare come from?
You who are so quick to judge?
Do you have some yardstick of truth,
some treasure map of virtue?
Do you understand the ways of God?
        Do you whisper advice into his ear?

He must not be heeding your sage wisdom
for I am still here irking you with my
"strange and disturbing" behavior that
is so unlike your own untarnished form.
My ways are foreign to you and
        therefore must be wrong.

The baseline of your horror is that
you condemn what you do not understand,
you denounce what you do not know.
The things you do not like in me
are the things you do not like within yourself.
        You judge me to push away your vice.

But there are many stones in the pathway,
a variety of blossoms in the garden.
Many parts must make up the whole,
many colors are brushed upon creation's canvas.
We are not in a position to see the masterpiece
        as we are but a layer of paint ourselves.

So let us not point to the canvas with convictions,
stripping one another's being with ridicule and shame,
but may we rush to encourage each other's color,
to enjoy the contrast as we are bound together.
Let judgment lie in the hands of the Artist
        and let acceptance and appreciation lie in ours.

In His Eyes

Music All Your Own

Each life has a sound, a music all its own.
Some are drifting melodies played out on
the keys of a solo saxophone,
the notes of a piano
interwoven through their song.
Others are dancing the bamboula in
Congo Square to the Brazilian beat.
There are lilting Irish flutes
reminding us of the beyond,
and elegant harps pulling on their strings
keeping us mindful of what we were made to be.
Symbols suspended before the great crash,
oboes sweet and low, the passion of an opera—
the tearful notes of a soulful violin.
Do you hear the movements,
the soaring arias sung above life's stage?
The robust bassoons, electric guitars—
the sad and unplayed instruments of our time?
What does your life sound like?
What music are you composing?
Is it a steady rhythm or a beauty in the midst of fury?
And are you sitting by listening to what you hear,
or are you lifting up your feet
to step with the cadence of jazz?
Never shut the music in.
Whether it be a harmonious ballad
or a leaping Petrushka, open and boundless,
whatever your notes may be,
play them from your heart.

Zucchini

One little seed in the ground,
planted, watered, watched over,
but not by me.

Large and green it grows with each
foot long slice of God's provision
stretching out from the vine
toward my curious eyes,
my inquisitive fingers
lifting up the leaves in
amazed delight
that all these wonderful things
can come from one tiny seed.

Dancing down my garden path,
I wonder if my life
could be like the seed?

In His Eyes

Changing Clouds

White tufts of cotton
strolling through the blue expanse of sea,
skirting around the sun's bountiful rays–
a blanket covering the earth
wrapping the land in misty veils,
softly running down all below.
The clouds roll along
keeping time with changing life,
reflecting God in different ways.
All true, all connected into one circle,
the forebodingly dark thunderheads
to the peach ethereal haze,
magical places only those with wings know.
Yet we watch,
search the sky for understanding,
breathe in wonder and
exhale thanksgiving–
for these changing clouds.

Kairos...

...Are the moments in
your life that change
the way you live.
The ones when you know
you will never feel the
pulse of life the same,
the rhythm of your
breathing will not
return to what it was.
Do you walk forward
and ignore these moments,
pretending you never saw
the realm of possibility?
Or stop to gawk at it
then awkwardly move on
as you would a freak
show at the fair?
You could tread in the water
backwards, putting distance
between the unknown
and what you have always felt to be.
Or do you pass through
the portal with open eyes,
willingly letting the reality
you have thus lived
move and change,
mutating into something
you have never seen or
thought of before,
something wonderful and new?
What do you do with the
kairos moments in your life?

Dreams Unspoken

Can you tell me what you crave?
    The longings of your heart within,
    the thing of which you've been depraved,
    that magical gift you hope to win?
What miracle of God do you desire
    the gift you pray that he may give,
    the dream that brings the warmth of a fire
    as this silent wish you live?
Do not let folly rule your head
    for seeking it you'll go astray,
    keep your focus on Christ instead
    so you can stand on that last day.
Our heavenly Father knows your mind
    and knows just what you need,
    to your thoughts he is inclined,
    your dreams he will exceed.
So lift your hands and raise your voice
    in humbled prayer and joyful praise,
    depend on him, make God your choice,
    and trust his holy ways.

Power of a Word

One word holds
earth shaking power–
to bring a mountain
to eruption
flowing Gilead's balm
into the deserts of
parched throats,
drawing forth watery
expressions of return
telling us
just what kind of
living force
a word can have.

A Great Army

A great army rushes over the land
as a dam breaks spewing forth the water,
snapping trees, and cleansing the
earth of all the decay and ruin
that has held it prisoner for too long.
The time has come for soldiers
to stand together,
marching with one footfall
as the heavy beat
resounds in the deep.
Too long have the people
been captives to the
whims of the enemy.
Too long have they stood idly by
while their fields and homes
have been consumed in flames.
The time has come to
take up the sword.
The time has come to
put aside our differences,
to band together under one Captain,
under one battle cry.
The call has come to stand and fight together.
To live or die,
the banners have been raised high
over the ocean of souls.
At last, at last!

In His Eyes

Companions for the Journey

*We come together into his presence
as we wash each other's feet,
touching hearts through touching hands
when three united meet.*

Notes of Nourishment

Whispers of your voice,
  melodies of your spirit
    float in through my window
      while spirit-filled thoughts of comfort
        let me know I am not alone.

Notes of untold wisdom,
  a song of guidance
    flows through my soul
      as I feel your heart touch me,
        letting my hands fall to join yours.

Waves of your questions,
  rejoinder of your hope
    reflects in my mirror of perplexity
      as I feel the peace of one who has gone before,
        thankful to God for letting us walk together.

Knowing Enough to Trust

It's a stretch to trust you
with anything I'd say.
It's an internal battle
to say it anyway.

What if you don't like it,
what if I go too far?
What if I cross a line
and our friendship mar?

You see that it's a challenge
to redo what I have learned,
but all myself feels safe inside
and I know the thought's returned.

I never knew that honesty
could be this joyful thing,
but I have come to treasure
the gift of God you bring.

Learning to lean upon each other,
giving honor to the One,
living as he meant it to be,
following the example of his Son.

When we meet him, we'll understand
why he gave us friends,
but I think it's because he knew we'd need
someone to reflect him till the end.

In His Eyes

Divine Light

You remind me of our gracious Lord
and how it must have been
to grow by what he said
while spending time with him.
It seems to me the love he gives
is flowing from your soul
out into the world beyond
like a never-ending scroll.
I know it's not been easy,
you've had a bumpy road,
but you have let it refine you heart
and I'm sure the Lord is proud.
I can see him smiling down,
taking great delight
in his beloved child
as he sings to you at night.
Looking, you have seen,
his miracles on earth,
the light of your soul is one of them,
he is your priceless worth.
I can see him clearly,
his love is in your face,
you blend together beautifully,
you radiate his grace.
Meeting you is knowing him
and I rejoice to think,
that I am friends with both of you,
that we share this eternal link.
For soon upon one nearby day
eternity will be here,

and together we will praise him
as he wipes away our tears.
Love will be forever,
perfect and divine,
and what rejoicing there will be,
when he says that "You are mine."
The relationships that we have formed
will be honored up above,
because it has been through one another,
he has shown his love.

Mentoring Streams

Like clear streaming water
irrigating a farmer's field,
you pour out your lives
into the grateful life of another.
You show me the road
I have only begun to travel
and you point out the things
I have only begun to see.
By listening to your stories
and being encouraged by your words,
I have learned to thirst for wisdom
and the God who gives it.

Walking Blessings

There are some people in this life
  who carry God's light in their eyes,
with his love in their spirit,
his praises they cry.

They walk in this world
  to encourage us all,
friends who are faithful
who help when we fall.

Delights to behold
  like flowers blooming in spring,
a walk in the woods
as the nightingale sings.

They are the sweet smell of grass,
  the breeze on your face,
the feeling of awe
in a magical place.

These are his children,
  the blessings he gives,
so the beloved he holds
might truly life live.

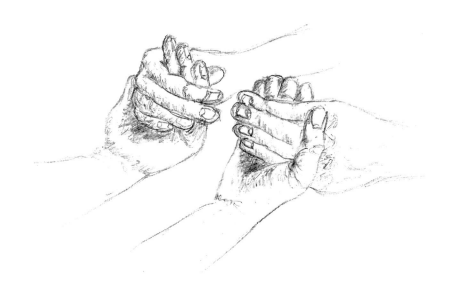

Carried in Prayer

Guided by the warmth of your hand
before our Father's throne,
you help me take the difficult steps
I fall from on my own.
The words you say–
they blow me away
as you thank him while I'm known.

Overcome I bow before him
beside you soul laid bare,
for three have come together
in the silence we have shared.
Through your tender words you've shown
that you are here, I'm not alone,
when you carry me in prayer.

In His Eyes

Intercessory Prayer

God, I come to you tonight
for a soul in need.
They are in a plight
and I know their heart you heed.
I can see you love them dearly
for when I gaze upon their face,
your love shines out so clearly
like a shining light of grace.
They have so much to carry Lord,
they bear a heavy load,
and their body is now weary
like a tree by wind now bowed.
Please come along their side
and hold their heart in yours,
give them rest while you abide
and open Heaven's doors.
Lord, they are your child
and beautiful to me,
grant them mercy mild
and peace upon the sea.

Your Touch

Today oh Lord I felt your hand
upon my shoulder here,
and it was a touch of grace
to remind me that you're near.
> When I felt your presence
> it took my breath away,
> and I looked around to see you
> to hear what you would say.

But I could never find you.
You could not be found.
I thought you must have slipped away
without making any sound.
> Then I saw your children
> standing right beside,
> and I could see you in their faces
> and your light shining from inside.

It was then that I discovered
you'd been there all along,
using their hands to touch my heart
and singing in their song.
> Now if I ever want to hear you,
> I know I can listen to their hymns,
> and if I ever want to see you,
> all I have to do is look at them.

Smile-Maker

Tiny spoons stir
little amber waves
as the pot is poured
into cheerful hearts
thirsty for
smiles exchanged
over steaming cups of tea,
the honey swirling down below
amidst the depth of conversation
forming a cherished sweet sip,
a warmth to be savored,
laughter to be shared
along with the scones
dripping with English jam
and clotted cream
edged with English lace.
What a gift of life to hold
like flowered teacups in your hand,
knowing you will think of this,
and smile once again.

Companions for the Journey

Let Us Plant a Garden

Let us plant a garden,
together you and I.
Let us cultivate the flowers
and watch them grow up high.

We'll walk among the leaves
whispering overhead,
looking out upon
where the lily blooms have tread.

Let me take your hand
as I walk here by your side,
loving you forever
as my darling bride.

Together we'll build a castle
with strong walls of our love,
and there will be shining towers
casting hope out from above.

Even though there will be storms,
our hearts will nearly break,
our love entwined will not unwind,
never shall we forsake.

When fifty years have come and gone
the walls will still be here,
and we will walk our garden
around our castle dear.

In His Eyes

I Give You the Daffodils

I walked in the woods
and what did I see,
a bouquet of flowers
waiting for thee.
Gold streaming yellow
and snow falling white,
the bright poppies orange
showered in light.

With green stems ablaze
reaching above,
waiting to tell you
of God's shining love.
They had bloomed in the ground
just for this day,
that I'd come along
and share what the Lord has to say.

He says that he loves you
and he'll always be there,
wanting to touch you
to show you he cares.
He wants you to come
and share what's inside,
he already knows
so you have nothing to hide.

His power is great
beyond all that is here,
and yet his heart breaks
when he sees your tears.
He says to remind you
his hand is in yours,
hold on to it tightly
and you'll feel yourself soar.

He told me to tell you
he's the fresh breath of spring,
he's the song of the birds
as they cheerily sing.
I then picked the flowers
to bring back to you
so I mayhap could share
this message I knew.

Christ used me to touch you
in this little way,
but the joy I received
is a star here to stay.
Like the flowers that bloom
I pray he'll pick me,
so he could then use it
as a blessing for thee.

For you to see Christ
in this life that I live
would be my great treasure,
the great gift God can give.
So I lay down my self,
held in God's power,
sharing his love
like the bright yellow flowers.

Voices of
Intimate Prayer

Sitting in the presence of my Father,
my soul within I share.
He whispers how much I am treasured
as we rest in intimate prayer.

Pool of Thoughts

Questions
longing
desire for God,
trust.
Exploration
tenderness
blessing
prayer,
haunting me.
A look–
a thought…
in silence.
Open
raw,
vulnerable.
Truth
wisdom–
freedom.
God.

Value of Naught

Even a hole that is
nothing is something.
Though it has been
taken away,
its emptiness allows
the light within to
spill forth into the
world beyond.
And while the wood
burns, does it not
glow in glory,
sending forth warmth
and flickering brightness
to those who
walk in darkness?
And what of the dirt?
Is it not the very entity that
all things are
founded upon?
The trees and
all living things
find their nourishment
beneath them
amongst the soil.
These nonexistent and
dying things,
yet it is they I use to
show my face.
Can I not do the
same with you?

In His Eyes

Grant Unto Me

Oh Lord, I want to be
a loving representative
of your grace and mercy.
To humbly walk in the world
with hope, holiness of character,
and a wise heart.
Let me consider my words
before I speak them,
and to know your words
better than my own.
Grant unto me a sense
of your eternal, ever-present self
and guide me along
the path you have
created for my soul.
Help me to know we have
been brought together
in an unbreakable union.
Keep your face before me
so I may not waiver
when the storms arise
and the rain lashes
against our dreams.
Above all, give me the
longing to know you alone Lord,
so that one day
I may wake up in your arms and
find I have returned home.

At the Feet of Jesus

I took my troubles to the Lord
and laid them plaintively
at his feet.
Standing before me,
frankly I told him of my thoughts,
my conflicts, and my joys.
For if not to him, then who?
He knows me utterly,
is closer to me than I am to myself,
and a burden shared
is a burden lifted.
Why try to hide from the
sun in an open field?
Why dry off in the river?
If I must struggle,
then let it be in the
glorious throne room of
the Eternal.
Before his presence I can
hear his guidance or at least
behold his great light.
Though the words may be hard to find
or even to admit to myself,
they must be faced openly, honestly,
if I am to become who
he wants me to be.

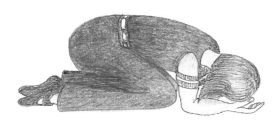

In His Eyes

Down Upon My Knees

So many things I don't understand,
sights I cannot see.
Fathoms deep within myself
as I go down upon my knees.
I ask the Father's council
and tell him what's on my mind,
I ask him for the wisdom he gives
and the answers I have to find.
He is always there to listen
and helps along the way,
he is there to see me through,
by my side he'll always stay.
So I bow my head in silence
lifting a prayer to up above,
he hears his child talking
and answers with his love.

Sacred Ground

I enter into your space
and remove my shoes
trusting that no entity around us
will injure me.
I remove my socks
to lay my soul bare before you
without any fear
of an upturned brow
or spirit-breaking rejection.
Tonight I come to you—
naked and exposed
for I am a child newly born
taking her first steps on sacred ground
soaked in prayer,
experiencing the warmth of your hand
as you lead me further on.

Everlasting Words

Abba Father,
I am exhausted from bearing
this immense pain inside of me,
unexpressed and hidden
for fear of being ignored,
or in trepidation of the look in their eyes
if they knew what dark rivers of dejection
flow underneath a barely calm exterior.
What would they say if
they knew how many invisible
tears fall from the wounds in my heart,
the ones you are wiping away day after day?
Can you just take the pain away?
Throw the black bundle of agony
into the eternal sea of forgetfulness?
I am ready to never know it was here.

My love, I know you do not want to
feel the ache of your pain,
that ever present reality you cannot
escape from no matter how hard you try.
I can feel your tears for I have cried them too,
and I have been there with you
as you have grappled to make sense of it all.
But I love you more than to
let you walk away from it as
if the darkness never happened.
I love you so much more than to
lct you cast your pain aside.
Casting your pain aside is not the answer.

Then what is the answer God?
You say you love me...
but then why am I here in

a room of nightmares I cannot escape?
Why are you not coming for me?
Don't you care?

Oh, my beloved one,
I do love you.
I love you so much that I choose
to be in that room with you.
I do not have to come for you
for I am already there holding you close
in the midst of the nightmares.
You see, not only do I love you,
but I respect you and I respect
all of the energy you have poured
into your pain and into fighting
the nightmares with your bleeding questions.
I won't throw something away
you have put so much of your heart into.

So you are just going to let me suffer
through this battle?
You are just going to hold me
when you have the power to
lay the nightmares flat on the ground
groveling at your feet?
That's all you do?
Where is the sense in that?
Where is the love in making me
breathe in the garbage life has handed out?

My precious treasure,
I would never leave you to battle
with the nightmares on your own.
This is my battle and I will fight it for you.
Just be still, go ahead and cry,

and know that I am here.
But you are right, there is no love
if I let the nightmares tear your soul apart,
yet they are too dear to throw away
since so much of you, whom I love,
is in them.
That is why I take the pain
into my hands to transform it
into something beautiful
that will make your life richer
and your eternal delights greater.
They will be like pearls around your neck,
particles of sand that once hurt you
but will be changed into exquisite
testimonies of our relationship.
This will be your inheritance,
the power of my love working
extraordinary miracles in the life
you wanted to throw away.
It is in your pain as well as your joy
that I am seen.
When you are empty, I will fill you,
and when you want to run away from
the life you know,
I will be running beside you
helping you to understand
I am not finished with you yet.
Wait and see and I promise
there will not be any tear
I will not use,
not one sigh will go untransformed
and you will finally see with what
inestimable worth I created you.
So hold onto me, keep talking,
and soon your sun will rise.

In His Eyes

Upon the Country Road

Carrying my travel-tattered bags
full of long forgotten mementoes,
I continue walking with dust upon my shoes
and a worn coat flapping in the wind.

Going I know not where,
from where I do not want to return,
I put my lone feet forward upon the trail
making my solitary journey through the valley of death.

Then I feel a touch upon my arm
and look to see a pierced hand
laid across my shoulder with a whispered voice,
"No, not alone, never alone."

Heart Tired

Where do you go God when I am heart tired?
I am here.
Where do you wander off to when I am alone,
surrounded by faces, exhausted by the demands?
I am here.
How can you not be there when my legs are shaking
and my eyes are watering from the strain to see?
I am here.
Why can you not come?
I am here.
Do you not care when I cannot go on?
Yes, I care.
Did you not say you would save me?
Yes, I will save you.
That you would snatch me out of the flames?
Yes, I will not let you burn.
But now as my knees fall to the ground,
I feel someone move underneath me and lift me up.
Is that you God?
Yes, it is.
Is that where you have been all along?
Yes, I am here.
Why could I not see you before?
Because I was carrying you.

The Great I Am's Delight

Do you not think I am pleased with you? I am.
What is wrong with being pleased with you? I am.
Sure you make mistakes and you aren't perfect,
but I don't expect you to be, I know.
But it is your heart that makes me proud,
your obedience.
I take great joy when you follow me,
letting me guide you;
when you depend on me for your life.
Yes, I am pleased with that.
Why do you argue against this?
Am I not free to be pleased with you?
Until you get this, you will always
try to be pleased with yourself,
you will always be trying to prove something.
But you don't have to prove anything to me.
I already like you. Who you are,
what you look like, and what you do.
Don't be so hard on yourself.
I would be a harsh God if I held your standards.
It's okay to try new things and make mistakes.
I enjoy watching you try.
Come to me now.
Let me touch you, let me enjoy you.
This is real,
more real than you know.
Someday I'll show you.
I'll show you just how real I am.
Until then, be happy with yourself and
know that I, the Creator of all you see
and the Knower of all you don't see, the One Mover,
Shaker, the One who controls all things, the Great King
with the world as his footstool,
am your biggest fan.

Where I Want You

I know you are tired and have
no strength left within you to go on.
I know you look at what is left to be done
and shrink back in overwhelming anxiety.
I know the heights you want to reach.
But you can't keep giving without letting me fill you up.
I know you are struggling to
do it all and to do it right.
But you don't do anything dear one—you let me.
I will do everything.
I will accomplish it with my own hands.
You do not need to fight,
I am here to take over.
Know this well, that I crossed the chasm
and I drank sin's poison.
I am the one who lifted you out of Satan's grave.
You were very passive in it all,
you accomplished nothing.
But what you do not yet understand is
that is where I want you.
I want you to be empty, drained,
unable to do things for yourself.
Without that, I cannot do them for you.
I cannot give you everlasting jewels if
you are grasping plastic beads.
So be content in your emptiness,
watch for me in your insufficiency,
and I will come to you,
and I will do all things.

Dancing His Praise

Dancing before the Father's throne,
embodying his praise,
reveling in his glory,
basking in his gaze.

Overflowing Praise

I come into your presence today El Shaddai
to offer you my humbled heart
for you are truly an awesome God
and are worthy of such marvelous praise.
I am so grateful for the grace
you have given me my Father,
so I would like to offer you the work of my hands
and the voice of my spirit.
Please use this, my soul-prayer
to shine forth your righteous light
to touch the lives of those you love,
those who you save with your mighty hand.
Today I raise my song and praise your being to the sky.
Hearing you call out my name Lord,
today I answer:

                  Here I am,

                      use me.

It's All for You

Tonight I bring you simple praise,
     my heart bowed down,
     my hands upraised.
Even though I cannot see
     where you are
     or where you'll be,
I trust in you because I know
     you are there
     above, below.
You are the King, you are the One,
     you are the light
     of Heaven's sun.
And though I may not understand,
     I've made my choice,
     I'll take my stand.
Though the world may seem heavy and grey,
     to you the darkness
     is bright as day.
You see much more than I do here,
     you'll guide my soul,
     you're always near.
For you are greater than I am,
     you the slain,
     the bloody lamb.
I'll trust your way to make me new,
     I cry out loud,
     "It's all for you!"

So Richly Blessed

Oh wilt thou train my ear to hear
thy quiet voice when I draw near,
    the time when I lay down to rest,
to see thine face when mine eyes close,
finding you in sweet repose.
    Ah! That I would be so richly blessed!

What midnight sun shall we behold
when at last our hearts enfold
    into thine One, upon thy breast
where we are whole and sinless free
as thine redeemed are united to thee!
    Ah! That we would be so richly blessed!

Take our hands, let them serve
as thy light for you deserve
    all our praise, our crowns, our best,
as on that day when trumpets ring out,
on knees we'll fall and we will shout,
    "We as thy people, so richly blessed!"

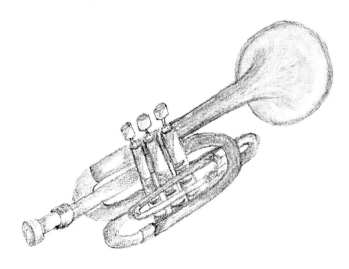

Dancing His Praise

Holy Flair

Leaning against
the pasture gate,
the sky alit, ablaze,
with my eyes agape in wonder
standing humbled and amazed.
Words step back
before the proof
of your power in the sky,
as I sense you step beside me
to see the sunset nigh.

My eyes explore
the glowing colors
reflected on your face,
I then gaze back into the stage above
to watch the play of grace.
Lord, the power
that you hold
is beyond what I can know,
as I am held in awe
before your fire show.

You have got
a sacred style
that takes my breath away,
and I am filled with love for you
as I've caught a glimpse of you today.
But the deeper
wonder of it all
is when it's me you see,
for you see beauty beyond compare
because you shine through me.

In His Eyes

Thanks for You

What a joy it is to tell you
the goings on today,
because you will always listen
for you are here to stay.
I cannot step over a line
where you no longer are,
accepting me just as I am
like the morning stars.
You are ever here beside me,
your mercy is ever new,
your tender heart enfolds me
with everything that's true.
It's such a comfort for me to know
that I don't have to "do",
but that you love me because I'm yours
and accept me through and through.
It doesn't matter what goes on,
it's fleeting and will pass by,
your love is forever
and will continue when I die.

Rejoice!

What a kind God you are!
You give refreshment to those
who are thirsty.
You give rest to those
who are weary
and in the morning dawn
you bring great joy,
contentment for today
and hope for tomorrow.
You renew our souls.
What a great God you are!

Jehovah

With you I can laugh again.
With you the world is good.
And even if it isn't good,
even if it is a bitter ale to swallow,
you are good,
and that makes all the difference.

Stumbling Steps

Father, if you can use a
faltering voice like mine,
I will sing praises to your name.
If you can use my stumbling steps,
I will try to take them all toward you.
If you want to use my broken body,
my limited vision, or my shaking hands,
I will lift them up in prayer.
For in you everything is redeemed,
everything is made new,
everything is transformed,
even me,
        in you.

He Has Brought Me

He has brought me
who was hungry
up to his feasting table.
He has brought me
who was thirsty
to his everlasting fountain.
He has brought me
who was alone,
who was tired,
who had no hope save his,
into his gentle care
and holy calling.
He brought me
        because he bought me.

Beyond What I Can See

I stand trembling before your throne
    for you are worthy of praise alone.
You are God and you are King,
    you are the One to whom I sing.
I love to look into your face
    and see your glory within this place.

Forgive me if I've lost the view
    and made a distorted picture of you.
Please excuse my finite human mind
    when I judge you by the faults I find
within the hearts of those I know,
    those with whom the hurtful go.

But I yearn to know who you really are,
    who formed the earth and hung the stars,
who lights the sun by his infinite power,
    yet watches over the tiniest flower.
Tell me what it is you want me to see
    as I am here on humbled knees.

In the past, I have confined
    you to a box as I've been blind,
but now I want your healing hand
    and I don't want to understand,
because I'd rather depend on your voice
    by making faith my final choice.

So with my head bowed, my hands raised high,
    I will shout your glories and cry,
and although I rejoice to eternally love
    you my God so high above,
you will always be teaching me things that are new
    that I may never underestimate you.

In His Eyes

Lost in Wondrous Delight

Delighting in a squirrel
peeking out from within a tree,
enjoying the world around us
as we glimpse eternity.

Sunshine on My Road

Doggie kisses in the morning,
notes singing underneath the
warmth of my hand,
a work well done,
hydrangeas in bloom
are the sunshine on my road.

The threads in a quilt,
a nap in the park then
floating in a lake,
tapping out the beat,
the company of a friend
are the sunshine on my road.

A quiet evening in a book,
standing on the shore of the sea,
sand between my toes,
then gazing upon the star filled sky
while breathing in the breath of my Creator
are the sunshine on my road.

What I Live For

I live for my teddy
who sits on my bed,
and for the blue corduroy hat
that's perched on my head.

I live for the daffodils
that bloom in the spring,
and for the shiny brass bells
that cheerily ring.

I live for the books
with knowledge inside,
and for all the tall trees
with the chipmunks they hide.

I live for the sea,
the roar of the waves,
and the seashells I see
by the sea lion's cave.

I live for the little things
that mark each new day,
and for our God up above
who made it that way.

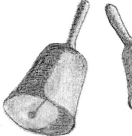

In His Eyes

Falling Leaves

Falling leaves float to the ground
lighting on my outstretched hand.
The breeze, swirling around
my transported figure,
tousles my burnished hair
up into the air along with the
orange and red creations
twirling one after the other
through the sparkling shower
of beauty by which the leaves and I are held.
Both of us moving to an unknown
but glorious end,
an end that doesn't really end,
but an end that leads to beginnings.

Laughing Without Fear

Held up in the wonder of God's hand,
the water falling on my outstretched arms
as I climb around his wonders
and hop along the stones in the
cooling stream of refreshing vitality.
I learn to laugh again, to laugh with no fear
as if everything inside me was
bursting with child-like jubilation
while bouncing on the bouncy log–
up and down, up and down!
Then to see my abundant joy
reflected in another's eyes–
another of God's created ones
who sees me as I am
and laughs with me once again.

Lost in Wondrous Delight

What is Art?

Art...
Dare you define it?
Is it line or color,
    a woman smiling?
    Architectural design
        or the graffiti as it
    passes by you on the train?
Does it consist of
    oil paint or dappled glass,
    a Moroccan castle in the east?
Or does it have morality at all?
    Can it be good or bad,
        mean spirited or made in
            righteous anger?
Art for art's sake or something else...
Perhaps it makes people see
    something common in a new way,
    or it could be an invitation.
Can art be a green board
    reclined against the wall?
    What does that say?
Is it golden toned landscapes
        falling down from their frames,
    or statues dancing in the paint?
There is genius to offend, to teach,
    to show us beauty we had missed.
What does art mean for you?

Nurturing Creation

To think that I have the humbling honor
of sharing in your creative work
by the tending of my hands
into the fertile soil beneath my knees,
a soil saturated in abundant life and growth–
teaming with your bountiful handiwork
and basking in the warmth of your glory.
The flowers exude your fragrance,
the sweet pine aroma laced with blackberries
reminding me of your vast outlook
over all the feather-leafed textures of the earth
while the peach poppies run in the valley
and the violet irises flow into one another
beside the river's crystal walk.
By nurturing and caring for such
rich and radiant splendor,
I have shared a part in bringing forth
a reflection of your beauty
that mirrors your compassionate heart
even as I create a nourishing world for a bee.
Traversing these trails
in my garden,
I pray I leave them
richer than when I came.
Having walked with the
movements of the earth,
you will in turn sustain me with
your bountiful harvest
and I will sing your
praises with the trees.

Quilting

Contrasting colors and textures
joined together to form
a cohesive whole of shared lives
into a quilt of many colors.
Running hands across
the varying fabrics,
soft beneath the touch,
watching variances come together
into one beautiful design.
The scraps creatively
connected to one another
into an emerging pattern
bound together by the
infinite blue around its borders
and the sun-shining yellow
speckled throughout–
as if to say there is always
light amidst the dark.
Treasured for its imperfections
where red corners don't meet green,
the stitches out of place–
uniqueness, grace, and value
is brought together from what was
previously seen as wrong,
in actuality—quite right.
Then on stormy winter nights,
the soul wrapped in warmth,
a sense of safety and protection
given by all the loving hands
and the Hand that made it.
This delight, creating something new
from the throwaway pieces–
could that be how God feels about us
and our broken spirits?
What beauty does God see in the quilts of our lives?

In His Eyes

Tickles and Tea
For Ellie

Crouched behind the chair,
I lie in wait for you to come.
"Sarah, where are you?" soon
followed by, "I'm coming to find you!"
wafts down the hall as
I try to stifle my giggles.
And when your delightful grin
finally appears with mock rebellion
inducing me to tickle you,
you put up a valiant struggle
only betrayed by the mischievous
glint shining from your eyes.
In your room
hiding underneath the blanket,
you tell me the things
Heaven only whispers
through the young
as we sing the nursery rhymes
and repeat the stories
etched into your mind.
Who else would think of picnics
with fish crackers, or laugh
uproariously at my dancing?
My adult solemnity abandoned,
we indulge in ruckus
piggy-back rides

and adventures in play dough.
At tea time you tell me what you created
but before I can tuck in,
you take my hand and declare,
"We need to pray."
Appropriately corrected,
we take hands to go to God.
I wonder just who is the teacher?
Now while I kneel before you as
you run into me with open arms,
his words, "And a little child shall lead them,"
come to mind, then I take you
up into my arms for a hug and
all else lies forgotten.

Coffee House

Sprawled upon the pillows
looking all around,
pencil ready in my hands
listening to the sounds
of coffee grounds a-pounding
and the barista crushing ice,
the parade of people's voices
and the smell of eastern spice.
A man who does the crossword
with glasses in his hand,
the scuffing of the chairs
as a group of friends disband.
Lights that cast their shadows
toward photos on the wall,
barrels stacked up overhead
that look like they will fall.
Then the final call goes out
as the bagels are disposed,
"Come on back tomorrow,
the Coffee House is closed."

Tapping Time

I never knew I'd have such fun
shuffling off to Buffalo,
        but every time I flap ball-change,
I stamp and stomp and know
        that this is where I'm meant to be
as the steps together flow
        into a mamba grapevine
so we can get our kicks,
        while digging our toes and dropping our heals
in the song "Route 66"–
        then on and on the riffles come,
each tap shoe sounding clicks.
        Sambas echo on the wood
as our feet find rhythmic rhyme,
        delight shining forth from within our eyes
as at last it sounds sublime.
        We are our own dancing stars
when we come to tapping time!

Lost in Wondrous Delight   135

Theatre Seats

Oceans of heads and waves of bodies
discovering new viewpoints as they sink
into the deep crimson seats of the mezzanine,
gothic arches soaring high above in the air.
Peering over the balcony rail into the sea below,
they finger their programs to preview
the spectacular spectacle soon to come
as eager faces betray their excitement within
looking expectantly for the fabric door
to usher them into a world waiting to be tasted
and savored for every morsel of art
delectably served up before their hungry eyes.
Dark night soon descends with a hush
and every soul shifts their gaze to the
golden tassels lifting off the stage floor
in dramatic flair revealing the web of fantasy
woven for the viewer with creative wings.
Bodies hanging in the air in graceful movement–
dancer's arms soon singing to the beat of the music
as feet sweep the floor and point up in the air
in expressions hitherto unknown, newly admired.
Collective intakes of breath punctuates each feat
of balance-defying shows of beauty and collectiveness,
leaving the viewers in mutual wonder and astonishment
over such poignant demonstrations of the
passion within each performing spirit
to tell the story best told in words colored
by pulsating hands and arched backs.
The audience now transported into timeless ecstasy,
only one second to glance back to the reality before
to know the world illustrated before their senses
has now transformed something deep within them,
reflecting the magnificence now intimately experienced,
leaving them forever changed and forever new.
What a dance, what a night!

In His Eyes

Twilight

Lying upon my back in the hayfield
watching the fiery streaks
of pink clouds blooming against the scene above,
I ponder the ever deepening mysteries of color
as orange transforms to blazing red
and the green of the maple
seems to glow from within.
Drifting into the peace of Heaven's glory,
roving along an indigo sea
over the vast expanse of air,
my heart settles into the moment,
treasuring it for the wonder moments are.

Epilogue: In His Eyes

Hearing your beloved voice,
   I look into the sky
and then the world stops spinning
as I sink into the deep
   centrality of your eyes.

Nothing more gives me lasting peace
   or opens up a wider view
than when I look up to see your face
and I sense your love
   amidst the wonder I find in you.

You have become my life-force,
   all glory to your name.
I am merely your creation,
treasured and cherished,
   but a reflection just the same.

Then sometimes when I don't understand,
   I know that you're still here.
For you said you would never leave me,
that you will always be my guide,
   to walk with me far and near.

The beauty and power of the universe
   is your majesty revealed,
yet you love me beyond words,
paid the price and drew me to you
   so through your eyes I now stand sealed.

All glory be to you our God and Savior.
You are before beginnings and the One who never ends.
All our praise we lay before you
as we joyfully shout your name to the heavens.

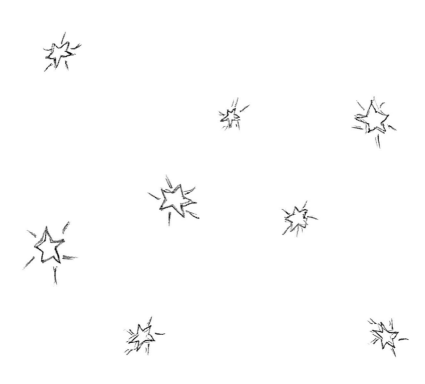

About the Author and Illustrator

Sarah Katreen Hoggatt, the author, has been writing creatively for over nineteen years and loves the idea of painting art by using words. She is a freelance writer, speaker, editor, visual artist, and spiritual director with a passion for ministering to searching souls. She holds a Master of Arts degree in Christian Ministry and a Certificate of Spiritual Formation and Discipleship from George Fox Evangelical Seminary in addition to her Bachelor of Science degree from Oregon State University. Sarah currently makes her home in Salem, Oregon where she enjoys the theatre, photography, hiking, and creating things with her hands. She is passionate about living her life as a gift.

ClaraLee Esther, the illustrator, is an artist who uses many different mediums; her abilities have been cultured through several college classes. She also writes poetry, is an avid journaler, and collects books. Her life's twin callings of nature preservation and ministry to the grieving are both passions which are close to her heart. ClaraLee lives in Independence, Oregon, with her beloved husband, Bill, with whom she has raised

seven children and now enjoys twenty-one grandchildren. The Lord has always been present in ClaraLee's life and the life of her family; she firmly believes that we are the hands and feet of Jesus on this earth. Mother Teresa said, "Love is the golden chain of all virtues...small things done in great love bring joy and peace."